BRIGHTON IN COLOUR

A SOUVENIR GUIDE

Photographs by
ERNEST FRANKL

Text by
ANGELA FIDDES

THE PEVENSEY PRESS
Cambridge England

Front cover: The Royal Pavilion from the Steine.

Back cover: Tombstone of Martha Gunn, St Nicholas' churchyard. Born into an old Brighton family, and one of the original 'bathers' or 'dippers', whose job was to hold people while they bathed in the sea, Martha Gunn became a celebrated local figure, to be seen even during the last days of her life (she lived to be 89) on the beach, acting as a superintendent. She was reputedly a great favourite of the Prince Regent, and the story is told that he met her one day in the Pavilion kitchens, and noticed that she had secreted a pound of butter in her pocket; to tease her, he started a long conversation with her, all the time edging her toward the fire, until a pool of melted butter lay on the floor.

Published by The Pevensey Press
6 De Freville Avenue, Cambridge CB4 1HR, UK

Photographs by Ernest Frankl except 4, 18: The Royal Pavilion, Art Gallery and Museums, Brighton.

Edited by Ruth Smith
Designed by Tim McPhee in association with The Pevensey Press
Design and production in association with Book Production Consultants, Cambridge
© Ernest Frankl, Angela Fiddes and The Pevensey Press, 1983

ISBN 0 907115 15 2

Typesetting in Baskerville by Westholme Graphics Ltd
Printed in Hong Kong

Contents

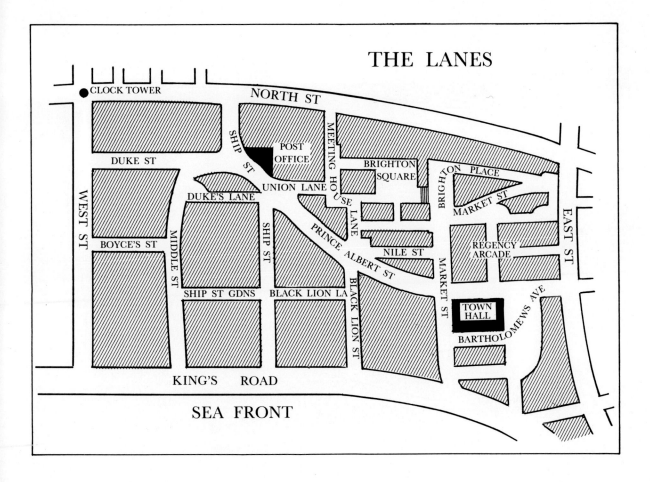

THE LANES

CLOCK TOWER

NORTH ST

WEST ST

DUKE ST

SHIP ST

POST OFFICE

MEETING HOUSE LANE

BRIGHTON SQUARE

BRIGHTON PLACE

UNION LANE

DUKE'S LANE

MARKET ST

EAST ST

BOYCE'S ST

MIDDLE ST

SHIP ST

PRINCE ALBERT ST

NILE ST

REGENCY ARCADE

MARKET ST

SHIP ST GDNS

BLACK LION LA

BLACK LION ST

TOWN HALL

BARTHOLOMEWS AVE

KING'S ROAD

SEA FRONT

From Prehistory to the Present

There have been settlements in and around Brighton since Neolithic times, early man preferring to live on high ground such as Whitehawk Hill or Hollingbury Hill, rather than the narrow strip of coastal plain where the modern town centre lies. According to local annals, in Saxon times Brighton was held by Ulnoth, grandfather of King Harold; but it is with the Domesday Book (1086) that our detailed knowledge of 'Bristelmestune', as it calls the settlement, begins. The town's name has changed more than once – for long it was known as Brighthelmeston, the modern form being officially established only in the early 19th century.

In 1086 'Bristelmestune' was a fishing community of about 90 people at the mouth of the Wellesbourne, paying the Crown an annual rent of 4000 herrings. The medieval town consisted of an upper part, inhabited by farmers and artisans, and a lower part, on the beach below the cliff, where fishing families lived. The church of St Nicholas of Myra, the patron saint of fishermen, was built in the 14th century to replace an earlier structure. Its site, on a high hill then outside the town, was chosen either as providing a landmark for sailors, or because of some former pagan association of the hill. Medieval Brighton seems not to have been particularly prosperous. Although in 1313 Edward II granted the right to hold a weekly market (on Thursdays) and a 3-day St Bartholomew fair, the townspeople claimed exemption from taxation in 1349 on the grounds that 'here are no merchants, but tenants of land, who live by their own hand and great labours only'.

The earliest map of Brighton supposedly depicts an attack by the French in 1545 (though it is not certain that this actually took place); it shows that East St, Middle St, West St and North St are survivals of the original rectangular Tudor layout. The area between Middle St and East St was known as the Hempshares: here hemp was grown for the fishermen's nets. Like other south-coast towns Brighton was vulnerable to attack and, in wars against France, to invasion. During the 16th century defences were organised, but not until the town had been almost wholly destroyed. In June 1514 French forces under the notorious admiral Prégent de Bidoux (known in England as 'Prior John') landed and fired the town, seizing what they could before being driven off by a local force hastily summoned by the lighting of beacons on the Downs. All the medieval buildings perished except St Nicholas' church, though the present-day Lanes give some idea of the layout and character of medieval Brighton. The townspeople continued to rely on fishing for their prosperity, and in the 1580s Brighton was one of the most important south-coast fishing ports, with 80 vessels, 400 fishermen and about 10,000 nets. There was always tension between the fishermen and the landsmen. In the 16th century the cost of defending the town fell mainly to the fishermen, who petitioned the Privy Council to spread the expense. As a result 'The Booke of Auncient Customs' was drawn up, detailing the organisation and financing of the local fishing industry, and a local government body was created – 'The Twelve' (8 fishermen and 4 landsmen) to assist in

◄ **1** *George IV by Sir Francis Chantrey (a copy in bronze of the marble statue at Windsor), erected on the Steine in 1828, the cost of £3000 being defrayed by public subscription. In 1922 the statue was moved to its present site by the North Gate of the Pavilion to make way for the War Memorial. George IV, who is inextricably linked with Brighton's rise to fame as a fashionable resort, ruled Britain as Regent from 1811 and became King in 1820, after one of the most magnificent and extravagant coronations ever seen.*

the enforcement of law and order, and to supervise repairs both to the church and to the town's defences. But the fishing industry began to decline in the 17th century, as local boats suffered harassment from foreign vessels and increasing competition from other British fishing fleets jealously guarding what they saw as their rights.

In 1657 occurred one of the most famous episodes in Brighton's early history, the escape of the future Charles II after his defeat by Parliamentary forces at the Battle of Worcester. Many stories have grown up around this event. Apparently Charles was brought here by Colonel Gounter, a local Royalist landowner, and Francis Mancell, a merchant from Chichester, who had persuaded a local shipowner, Captain Nicholas Tettersal, to carry 'two friends' of theirs – supposedly fleeing the country because of their involvement in a duel – to France for the sum of £50. The party spent the night at the now demolished George Inn, thought to have stood on the western side of West St – then a lonely part of the town, and so highly suitable. The innkeeper and Tettersal both recognised Charles, and it took much persuasion, and more money, before he was able to sail from the nearby port of Shoreham for Fécamp, in Normandy; only two hours later troops arrived in Brighton to search for him. After the Restoration of the monarchy in 1660, Tettersal was rewarded with a pension and made High Constable of Brighton, in which role he mounted a thorough and vindictive persecution of local Quakers and other Nonconformists.

In the 17th and 18th centuries the sea, ever a threat to the town, encroached even further inland, the worst damage being done in two terrible storms. The severity of the first, in 1703, led Daniel Defoe to write a treatise on storms which describes how in Brighton 'the violence of the wind stript a great many houses, turn'd up the leads off the church, overthrew two windmills . . . the town in general looking as if it had been bombarded'. In 1705 the lower town was totally destroyed, all its houses being buried under a mound of shingle, and the sea began to threaten the upper town. The only solution was to build wooden groynes which would cause an accumulation of protective shingle on the beach, but the population of Brighton was too impoverished to pay for them; so permission was granted for an appeal for funds to be made in churches and chapels throughout the county. The steadily decreasing population reached its nadir of around 1000 in 1740, and those who did live in Brighton were so poor that three-quarters of all houses were exempt from rates. There seemed a real possibility that the town might fall a victim to the sea when, by an ironic twist of fate, it was the fact that it was situated by the sea that led to Brighton's revival and transformation.

The first record of sea-bathing at Brighton comes from a letter of the Rev. William Clarke, who spent the summer of 1736 here with his family: 'my morning business is bathing in the sea . . .', he wrote to a friend. Nearly 20 years elapsed, however, before many people practised this novelty or, indeed, even visited the impoverished town. Then in 1750 Dr Richard Russell, from nearby Lewes, published *De Tabe Glandulari Sive De Usu Aquae Marinae In Morbis Glandularum Dissertio*. In this book he strongly advocated both swimming in and drinking sea water as a cure for various diseases, especially those affecting the glands. The medical profession was impressed (though the ideas were not entirely new), and when an English translation appeared, Russell's 'cure' became famous. Brighton being the nearest seaside town to Lewes, it was the destination of Dr Russell's patients.

▶ *2 St Nicholas' church, much restored in 1853, retains its 14th-century nave, chancel arch and tower. The interior contains several interesting memorials, including one to the Duke of Wellington, who went to school in Brighton. The chief pride of the church is its 12th-century font, an exquisitely carved piece of Caen stone, which possibly came from the Cluniac priory at Lewes to which Brighton was attached; this would account for the high quality of the work. The scenes depicted on it are the Last Supper, the Baptism of Christ, and episodes from the life of St Nicholas, one of them a delightful representation of the Saint in a boat, saving the lives of pilgrims by thwarting the approaches of the devil. In the churchyard are memorials to several well-known local figures, including Amon Wilds (see p. 13), Nicholas Tettersal (see p. 4), Phoebe Hassell (see p. 10) and Martha Gunn (see back cover). Brighton has some splendid Victorian churches too, notably St Michael's, Victoria Road, with windows by Rossetti and Morris, and the grandly proportioned St Bartholomew's, Ann St.*

Sea-bathing can hardly have been pleasurable when it was done, as most doctors recommended, early in the day during the winter; the novelist Fanny Burney, in describing her 'dip at dawn' on a November morning as 'cold but pleasant', explained that 'I have bathed so often as to lose my dread of the operation'. In those days very few people could actually swim, so they were always attended by a 'bather' or 'dipper', who would hold them and plunge them into the water from the steps of a bathing machine. Many of these attendants became well-known local figures, including 'Smoaker' Miles, the Prince Regent's bather, and Martha Gunn (see back cover). Six years before his death in 1759, Russell moved to Brighton; he had a house built at the south end of the Steine, where the Royal Albion Hotel now stands. His successors included Dr Anthony Relhan, who wrote a tract extolling Brighton's healthy climate, and Dr Awister, whose prescriptions included drinking a mixture of sea water and milk, and who had hot and cold sea water baths built in Pool Valley for those who could not face the rigours of the sea itself. It was during their time that Brighton began to emerge as a fashionable watering place, and soon both patients and ordinary visitors began to flock to the town in ever-increasing numbers. Its rising popularity was helped by its position as the south-coast town most accessible from London – though in the 1750s, reaching it by carrier's wagon could take two days. By the 1820s express coaches were accomplishing the journey in 5¼ hours.

Initially there was little for the visitors to do, and few places for them to stay

▲ 3 *Marlborough House (1769), now the Brighton Tourist Board's headquarters and architecturally one of Brighton's most important houses, was built by Samuel Shergold, proprietor of the Castle Hotel. The next owner, the Duke of Marlborough, sold it (1786) to William Hamilton, who employed Robert Adam to redesign it. The drawing room has a Sicilian marble fireplace and there is a charming octagonal dining room; the house is one of the few surviving examples of Adam's work on a small domestic scale.*

except small lodging houses owned by fishermen. The only hotels of any consequence were the Castle (now demolished) and the Old Ship, and both were quick to capitalise on the town's new popularity. By the 1760s both had Assembly Rooms, where balls and card parties were held under the auspices of the Master of Ceremonies appointed to organise the social life of the town during the fashionable season (June–September). The first and most famous Master of Ceremonies was Captain Wade, who also held the same position in Bath for several years. The visitors' pattern of life followed that of the spas of Bath and Tunbridge Wells. Apart from an early morning dip, a typical day's activities might include a public breakfast, a promenade along the Steine, and a visit to the library. This last was a very important aspect of Brighton life, corresponding socially to the Pump Rooms of the spas. The first libraries included Thomas' and Baker's; here subscribers would meet to read the papers, gossip, and – perhaps most important – study the lists of new arrivals in a book kept up to date by the Master of Ceremonies. The first permanent theatre was built in North St in 1774, the present Theatre Royal being erected in New Road in 1807. For the more energetic visitor, there was hunting on the Downs, or racing: the first organised race meeting took place in 1783, and the subsequent annual meetings were often attended by the Prince Regent. These and many other attractions drew all fashionable and literary society. The Thrale family had a house built in West St (now the site of Sherry's Dance Hall), and their visitors, besides Fanny Burney, included Dr Johnson – who however declared the place 'so truly desolate, that if one had a mind to hang oneself for desperation at being obliged to live there, it would be difficult to find a tree on which to fasten the rope'. The threat of war against France led to the establishment of a military camp just outside the town in 1793, adding to Brighton's liveliness and giving the feather-brained Lydia in Jane Austen's *Pride and Prejudice* cause to

➤ **4** *A model of a hog boat in Brighton Museum. 'Hoggies', used by mackerel fishermen, were developed to suit the conditions of the Brighton coastline in a form that could be easily launched off the shingle beach. Having a great deal of beam in proportion to their length, they were very stable even in rough seas. Hoggies were used in Brighton until the end of the 19th century, when the last one was burned on the beach at a 5th November bonfire.*

believe that 'a visit to Brighton comprised every possibility of earthly happiness', not least because 'that is the place to get husbands'.

Soon the Royal family was attracted to Brighton; it was to visit his uncle the Duke of Cumberland that the 21-year-old Prince of Wales first came here on 7 September 1783 – a cause for great local celebration and a tremendous welcome (marred by the death of a gunner firing the Royal Salute). It has been suggested that the Prince came to try sea-bathing as a cure for swollen neck glands. Whatever the reason, he was enchanted by the place, and his visits became a more or less annual event. Brighton's future prosperity was thus assured as it was now the semi-permanent residence of the heir apparent. The Prince was always popular locally, whatever feelings were about him elsewhere; his generosity to Brighton causes and people, such as the celebrated Phoebe Hassell, to whom he paid a weekly pension of half a guinea, was well known and appreciated. (Phoebe Hassell, who lived to be 108, had in her youth disguised herself as a boy and joined the British Army to be near her soldier lover, who had been posted to the West Indies. It was only after 17 years, when he was wounded, that she revealed her still undetected secret to the regimental Colonel's wife.) The Prince's birthdays were always marked in Brighton with bell-ringing, all kinds of races just outside the town, the roasting of an ox for the townspeople and a ball in the evening when the whole town was illuminated. For the Prince, Brighton provided the setting in which he could fully enjoy his new-found freedom from his parents and from the stuffy ways of the court at Windsor. His affairs with women were many and much talked about, none more so than his relationship with Mrs Maria Fitzherbert, a twice-widowed Roman Catholic, whom he secretly (and illegally) married in 1785. At Brighton they spent many of their happiest days, though always maintaining separate establishments.

Having decided that he wanted a permanent base here, the Prince commissioned the architect Henry Holland to design a residence for him. The Marine Pavilion, completed within 4 months in 1787, was a simple classical building in the Palladian style, with a central rotunda and bow-fronted wings to north and south. (It still forms the nucleus of the Pavilion, hidden by later building.) The Prince occupied rooms on the upper floor of the south wing, and reputedly had a reflecting glass fitted in his bedroom so that he could watch the comings and goings on the Steine while lying in bed. He was not long content with his new home, and additions and alterations were continually made, inside and out. In the 1800s the interior began to be refurbished in striking and fanciful Chinese style by Frederick Crace & Sons; in 1805 the great domed stables in Indian style (designed by William Porden) were erected (**17**), provoking the comment that the Prince's horses were better housed than he was himself. The style of the stables gave the Prince ideas for dramatic alterations to his Pavilion, and by 1815 he had sufficient resources. Of several architects who submitted plans John Nash was chosen to effect the transformation. By 1822 the building was in its present-day form. It contains a great mixture of styles, but the Indian inspiration clearly dominates; it is a building without parallel in this country, and contemporary reaction to it was at best mixed. William Hazlitt thought it looked 'like a collection of stone pumpkins and pepper boxes . . . anything more fantastical with a greater dearth of invention was never seen'. Several commented on the similarity with the Kremlin, in Moscow. The King (as he had now become) seemed pleased enough with his new home, though not with the

▲7   **8►**

Brighton and its surroundings offer constant delights to the lover of 18th-century and Regency architecture, from the grand sweeps of the crescents to varied details like the doorways shown here. **7** (above left): *Hillside is a handsome red brick Queen Anne house, architecturally the finest in the charming village of Rottingdean, a few miles east of Brighton. Its doorway is surrounded by a porch with Tuscan columns. In the years before World War I Hillside was leased by the actor-manager Herbert Beerbohm Tree, who entertained the leading figures of society, including Lady Diana Manners, the future Lady Diana Cooper.* **8** (above right): *10, Prince Albert St, also of red brick, is one of the few really spacious 18th-century houses in Brighton. The doorway is an excellent example of modern reconstruction, as is the whole of the ground floor.* **9** (right): *68, Ship St, like most of the houses in this street, also dates from the 18th century.*

cost of it (Nash had never presented an estimate), but in fact for the last few years of his life he spent much less time than formerly at Brighton. He always had a reputation for fast living and keeping unsuitable company, and inevitably stories of wild goings-on at the Pavilion began to circulate; but what the majority of eyewitnesses seemed to remark about an evening spent there was the intense heat of the rooms. Certainly Mrs Fitzherbert had a sobering influence on the Prince, but though he is said to have declared that she was the 'wife of his heart and soul' he twice abandoned her: in 1795, to marry Caroline of Brunswick, and again in 1811. She kept her house in Brighton, where she remained a popular figure, 'treated as a Queen', as the Whig politician Thomas Creevey remarked, 'at least of Brighton'. William IV was kind to her and offered to make her a Duchess. This she refused, but she did consent to her servants' wearing Royal livery. She died in 1837. Her monument in the Roman Catholic church of St John the Baptist, Bristol Road, shows her wearing the three wedding rings of her three marriages.

In 1791 the *Sussex Weekly Advertiser* declared, 'so great has been the increase of Company within these last few days at Brighton that there is not now a house on the Steine or on the Bank to be let', and the town spread as the annual number of visitors increased. Although Brighton is often described as a 'Regency' town, most building took place not during the Regency era but in the decade 1820–30, when the number of houses almost doubled. Much of this new building was the collaborative work of the local builder-architect Amon Wilds (born 1762) and C. A. Busby (1799–1834), who came to Brighton from a successful career in London and America. One of their first major projects was Thomas Read Kemp's grandiose scheme of Kemp Town (see **53**); other work included Brunswick Town (**45**) and much of Marine Parade (**52**). Meanwhile Amon Wilds' son, A. H. Wilds, working mainly on his own, designed much of Park Crescent, Western Terrace, and Montpelier Crescent (**47**). The architect of another important building dating from this period, St Peter's church (1824–8), was Charles Barry, who later designed the Houses of Parliament. St Peter's is one of the finest churches of the early Gothic revival. Originally built as a chapel of ease for St Nicholas', it became Brighton parish church in 1873.

The death of George IV in 1830 did little to diminish the popularity of the town. His successor William IV regularly stayed at the Pavilion with his wife Queen Adelaide, and they made additions to it in the form of the South Lodge, 'Queen Adelaide's Stables' in Church St (converted later into the present Art Gallery and Museum), and the North Lodge and Gate. One of William's favourite occupations was strolling up and down the newly erected Chain Pier, where he would stop to converse with some of his rather bemused subjects, and buy sweets for the children who followed him around. The Chain Pier (1823) was the first pier in Britain. Built as a landing place for the packet boats from France, it soon proved popular as a promenade for visitors. It was designed by Samuel Brown on the same principles as a suspension bridge, and stretched out to sea for 1134 ft. In December 1896, only 2 months after it had been declared unsafe and closed to the public, it was completely destroyed by a violent storm.

Queen Victoria and Prince Albert visited the Pavilion in their turn, but with little enthusiasm – partly because, as Victoria wrote to her aunt, 'the people are very indiscreet and troublesome here really, which makes the place quite a prison'. In February 1845 the Royal family left Brighton for the last time, and in future spent their holidays at Osborne House, on the Isle of Wight. Gradually all the Pavilion's furniture and fittings were removed to Windsor and Buckingham Palace, and it seemed likely that the building would be demolished. But the townspeople had grown attached to this odd structure in their midst, and opposed any such move. Eventually the local governing body, the Town Commissioners, acquired the Royal Pavilion for Brighton in 1850 for £50,000, a tiny fraction of what it had cost George IV. At once repairs and redecorations were effected, and in January 1851 a ball attended by 1400 people was held to celebrate the formal opening of the interior. The building was used for similar functions, as well as business meetings, concerts and lectures, for the next 100 years. Visitors continued to throng to Brighton, among them many of the famous writers and artists of the day: Thackeray, Dickens, who wrote much of *Dombey and Son* and *Bleak House* here, and Constable, who spent several summers here with his family between 1824 and 1839. He made a number of oil sketches of the coast and was evidently fascinated by the Chain Pier, which appears in *The Marine Parade and Chain Pier* (now in the Tate Gallery, London).

The railway between London and Brighton opened in September 1841, causing great local excitement and celebration. The first excursion train ran from London at Easter 1844, carrying hundreds of day trippers to the seaside in about 4½ hours. This was the start of the tourist phenomenon that reached its height in the 1860s, when the Whit Monday of 1862 saw about 130,000 visitors descend on Brighton – a not entirely welcome development. Many felt that the trippers did the town little good, sitting on the beach for most of the day and spending what little money they had on drink. But a new era was clearly dawning. Brighton was no longer a select watering place, but a seaside town where people came to enjoy themselves. Soon all manner of amusements were

▼ **11** *The beach first thing in the morning, with only a few hardy swimmers taking an early dip. Although it is mainly shingle, this 7-mile beach has always been one of the main attractions of Brighton and Hove, and on sunny days it quickly fills up with people of all ages, building sand castles, paddling, taking boats out, swimming, water-skiing, windsurfing, or just sitting in deck chairs sunbathing.*

12 *No seaside town is complete without sweet shops, and the ones along the Brighton seafront make dazzling displays of their brightly coloured and packaged wares – especially sticks of rock, which one shop advertises in over 40 varieties. Another shop claims to have been 'By Appointment to Charles II', in business as the Royal Sweetmakers since 1672.*

catering for them: the West Pier (1866); the Palace Pier (1899), replacing the Chain Pier; the highly popular Aquarium (opened 1872); and Volk's Railway. This was the first (1883) regular electric train service in Britain, albeit a short one – originally along the shore between the Aquarium and the Chain Pier. It was the brainchild of Magnus Volk, a Brighton man, who was also the first person to install domestic electric light and a telephone system in the town. He achieved his great aim of extending his railway to the nearby village of Rotting-dean in 1896; so that the train could run whatever the state of the tide, it was mounted on stilts 24 ft high, earning it the name of 'Daddy Long Legs'. Tourists loved it, but eventually this part of the line had to close, giving way to the construction of groynes to prevent cliff erosion. The railway still operates along the front (Palace Pier to Black Rock Pool), from April to September.

In Victorian times as now, the beach was the main attraction – though most people sat on it fully clothed, there being no such thing as swimwear, and bathing machines being expensive and over-subscribed (bathing machines continued in use until Edwardian times). A distinction developed between the noisy, crowded centre of the town, around the Chain and later the Palace Pier, where the trippers tended to congregate, and the more refined western end of the town, where the fashionable hotels were situated; some of the most particular visitors moved even further west into Hove, which in the 1890s established itself as a suburb for the affluent retired. After a period of depression in the first years of the 20th century, when the upper classes virtually deserted Brighton, the regular visits of Edward VII made the town fashionable again. In

1908 the luxury train The Southern Belle started to run between London and Brighton, and in September 1910 the list of visitors included 5 Dukes, 4 Duchesses, 1 Marquis, 23 Earls, 33 Barons and all the principal members of the Cabinet. The advent of the motor car also boosted the town's fortunes, Brighton being a good distance for a day trip from London. The trials and tribulations of these early vehicles are commemorated in the annual veteran car run, and were immortalised in the film *Genevieve*.

During World War I Brighton became a haven from the air raids on London, and for the wounded: at George V's suggestion the Pavilion was used as a hospital for Indian soldiers, and over 4000 had been treated there by April 1916. The commemorative South Gate of the Pavilion was erected as the gift of the Indian people in 1921. During World War II the threat of invasion was once again very real; the beaches were mined and wired off, the piers were blown up in the middle, and visitors were barred from the town, which wore a strange deserted air. Between the wars Brighton gained rather an unpleasant reputation as the centre of ruthless, underworld gangs (luridly portrayed in Graham Greene's *Brighton Rock*), which culminated at a Lewes race meeting in 1936, when the gangs were finally beaten after a fight between the police and the notorious Hoxton Mob. Violence returned to Brighton in the 1960s, this time on the beaches, with the seemingly ritual Bank Holiday clashes between the rival gangs of 'Mods' and 'Rockers' – now a thing of the past.

Brighton in the 20th century has also faced the conflict, common to many historic towns, between preservation and progress. Much of the building before 1945 was haphazard, and it was to oppose such developments as Embassy Court, a towering block of flats right next to Brunswick Terrace, and to ensure

▼ **13** *Sussex University: the Engineering and Applied Sciences building. The 200-acre campus, near the village of Falmer, is planned as a series of related zones linked by footpaths, with buildings grouped round informal courtyards – sciences to the east and arts and social sciences to the west. The distinctive architecture is unified by the use of local materials, especially a russet brick, and is sensitively accommodated to its beautiful parkland setting in the South Downs. Sir Basil Spence was the architect of the first buildings and of much of the layout.*

14 *Preston Rock Gardens. Brighton is justly proud of its fine municipal parks and gardens, which cover 3000 acres. These beautifully tended rock gardens, their subtle colours contrasting with the bright flowerbeds on the opposite side of the London Road, are in Preston, to the north of the town. Now totally engulfed by Brighton, this was once a separate village called Prestetone, meaning a priest's holding, and belonged to the Bishopric of Chichester.*

the preservation of Brighton's historic buildings, that the Regency Society was formed in 1945. Even in the 1930s the Pavilion was threatened with demolition, but restoration under the energetic guidance of successive Keepers, helped by the permanent loan by the Royal family of much of the original furniture, has returned it to its former glory and made it Brighton's greatest architectural attraction (**15, 18**). More than any other seaside town Brighton has coped with the competition to its tourist trade offered by cheap continental travel, creating new attractions (see p. 52) and developing in other areas. It has become the home of many London commuters, among them several well-known actors and actresses including, at one time, Laurence Olivier and Joan Plowright. The University of Sussex, granted its charter in 1961, is one of the major employers in the county. Besides being the first of Britain's post-war universities, it pioneered the adoption in England of broadly based undergraduate courses, in which students work within different schools – European, Afro-Asian or American – rather than single subjects. In 1982 there were 4500 students, many of them renting rooms in Brighton formerly taken by holidaymakers and doing much valuable voluntary community work. The excellent programmes of the University's Gardner Arts Centre, open to all, greatly enrich the cultural life of the area. The proliferation of language schools in the 1970s also served to diversify and strengthen the local economy. Through the centuries Brighton has adapted well, if sometimes by accident, to new challenges, while retaining its unique charm. It remains what Horace Smith so rightly dubbed it, 'the Queen of Watering Places'.

A Tour of the Centre

English interest in India and its culture, which had been growing since the early 17th century, was stimulated from 1795 by the publication of Thomas Daniell's series of views, *Oriental Scenery*. This showed the English the great beauty of Mughal Indian buildings, which provided the dominant inspiration for Nash's remodelling of the Prince Regent's Pavilion in 1815. (A notable earlier attempt to emulate the Indian style, Sezincote (1805), near Moreton-in-Marsh, Gloucestershire, was in part Thomas Daniell's creation and may have influenced the Prince, as he was a visitor there.) The Pavilion's entire eastern front, along the Steine (**15**), was clothed with an oriental colonnade, the columns being linked with Indian 'jalis' of pierced stone latticework; this and the continuous cornice of the Indian battlements give the building a sense of unity. The west front is perhaps less dramatically lovely, but has its own charm with its irregular outline. The large central Indian dome and the pair of smaller ones flanking it have been the subject of many jibes, but their squat form is offset by the minarets – some decorative, some disguised chimneys – which fill up every spare space on the roof. The last part of the Pavilion to be completed, the north front, housed the King's apartments and accommodation for visitors; it has a very neat outline with balconies and an Indian colonnade. The Pavilion was built of Bath stone and brick covered with stucco. Nash's innovative use of the new medium of cast-iron for the internal support of elaborate stonework has over the years caused problems, in that the iron rusts and corrodes the stone, which is now undergoing repair and conservation.

The colourful Pavilion Gardens (**16**) provide the opportunity to relax in tranquil surroundings only a few yards from the town centre and enjoy such traditional seaside entertainments as brass band concerts and, occasionally, Punch and Judy shows. There were pleasure gardens here in the late 18th century, the Brighthelmston Pleasure Grove, a venue for public breakfasts, concerts, races and firework displays.

The Dome (**17**), built 1803–5, formerly the Prince Regent's riding stables, takes its name from its enormous central cupola. This measures 85 ft across and 65 ft in height, and represents a remarkable engineering feat for its day: indeed at the time it was widely believed that the whole building would collapse. The architect, William Porden, drew his inspiration from the Cornmarket in Paris and the Great Mosque in Delhi. Forty horses were housed in stalls in a great circle, with a pool and fountain for watering them in the centre; in a balcony were harness rooms and accommodation for grooms and coachmen. Nowadays the Dome is used for conferences and concerts. It seats over 2000. The Riding House (10,000 sq ft), behind the Dome, built at the same time for the Prince to exercise his horses, became the Corn Exchange in the late 19th century and is now an exhibition hall.

The Banqueting Room (**18**), the climax of the Pavilion's interior transformation in thorough-going Chinoiserie, was chiefly designed by Robert Jones. Its rich colour and opulence, especially by contrast with the approach from a low and rather dark corridor, is spectacular. The ceiling, a 45-ft dome, is painted a vivid blue, against which lies the foliage of a plantain tree, partly modelled in copper. From this hangs a gilt dragon which carries a huge gasolier, 30 ft high and a ton in weight, with more dragons radiating from it. (In William IV's reign the gasolier was taken down after Queen Adelaide had a dream about it crashing to the ground.) In each corner of the room smaller gasoliers hang from the Fum, a legendary bird of Chinese mythology, one of the four symbolic figures which kept guard over the Empire. The walls are painted with 'Chinese scenes', framed in red and yellow blind fret; the window draperies were deep crimson satin tinged with gold; and the canopied ceilings at either end of the room were decorated in gold with birds, flowers and dragons hanging from the roof.

44–45, Old Steine (**19**), recently refurbished as offices, are among the few late-18th-century houses in the Steine to survive with little alteration. They are fronted with the black 'mathematical' tiles characteristic of many houses in Brighton. These look like shiny black bricks, but are in fact small facing tiles hung on a wooden frame, and are used on seaside houses because they resist sea spray and harsh winds much better than ordinary bricks and tiles.

The Steine (*steine* is Scandinavian for a stone), formerly common land where fishermen dried their nets and beached their boats during storms, became the fashionable promenade in the 18th century. Its enclosure in the 19th century caused angry demonstrations by the fishermen, who felt they were being deprived of their ancient rights. As the town spread east and west during succeeding years the Steine lost some of its identity as Brighton's focal point, but despite heavy traffic it retains, with its shady walks and colourful flowerbeds, an atmosphere of genteel urban leisure. Steine Gardens (**20**) are dominated by the sparkling fountain designed by A. H. Wilds, who was responsible for much of Brighton's early-19th-century architecture. The lower base of its elaborate structure rests on the entwined figures of three dolphins, which also form part of the coat of arms of the Borough of Brighton.

The Palace Pier was designed to replace the old Chain Pier, which the new West Pier had overtaken as a fashionable attraction. Although building started in 1891, it was not complete until 1899, by which time the Chain Pier had been destroyed by a storm (1896). The new pier was an immediate success with visitors, and has remained so, being thought by many to be the finest ever built. Its oriental domes and delicate filigree-work arches clearly show the influence of the Pavilion on its design. Initially every arch and roof-line was illuminated by electric lights, but after World War II (during which the pier was partly destroyed as a defensive measure) not all of these were replaced. The pierhead platform, with an ornate theatre, was added in 1901 and improved in 1911, when a bandstand and winter garden (now the Palace of Fun) were also constructed. The Palace Pier Repertory Company presented a wide and varied programme until lack of support forced it to disband in 1964. The theatre now houses the National Museum of Penny Slot Machines, and is full of the gadgets that delighted people at the turn of the century; for one old penny (available at the Museum) you can see 'Two Lovely Ladies' or 'What The Butler Didn't See'. The pier has always offered promenaders a wide variety of amusements and today you can still sample many traditional seaside delights here – buy whelks and mussels, candy floss, sticks of rock and all sorts of souvenirs, have your palm read by a clairvoyant, have your photograph taken with a marmoset, catch a fish, take a ride on the ghost train, or just enjoy a walk in the bracing sea air.

21: The pier from the beach to the west; **22**: the entrance – the original entrance of three arches in delicate ironwork was replaced in 1930 by the present entrance and clock-tower, when the Aquarium was rebuilt and the sea road widened; **23**: strolling down the west side of the pier. OVERLEAF: **24**: the Palace of Fun; **25**: the view from the end of the pier, east toward Kemp Town and Black Rock; **26**: looking west towards the West Pier; **27**: the end of the day, cleaners in the tea room.

21

22 23▼

The Lanes (see map on p. 1), the centre of medieval Brighton, were formerly a series of ill-lit narrow alleyways, known locally as twittens. Now they are lively and bustling, one of the most visited parts of Brighton. The narrow streets with overhanging upper stories, full of antique shops, jewellers, boutiques and craft stores, give a feeling of the old town, though most of the buildings date from the 19th century. Brighton Place, a small square to the north of Market St, formerly called The Knab (Scandinavian for a hill, or piece of rising ground), was the site of the town well and the venue for town meetings. Many of the cobble-fronted houses round the square have been demolished, but the old flint-fronted inn, the Druid's Head, a favourite resort of fishermen, still survives.

English's Oyster Bar (**28**), the celebrated fish restaurant at the entrance to the narrow alleyway of Market St, is one of the many Regency houses in Brighton to have had its ground floor altered to form shop windows, whilst retaining bays and other Regency features in its upper floor. In Edwardian times this was called the Cheeseman's Oyster Bar and was run by two imperious sisters. Smoking on the premises was strictly forbidden, as it might spoil the flavour of the oysters, and when Edward VII entered the restaurant one day smoking a cigar the sisters refused to serve him until he had put it out – which he did without protest.

The Bath Arms (**29**), at the corner of Meeting House Lane and Union St, one of the many popular drinking places in the Lanes, was built in the 1860s and has been restored to its original appearance, recreating its Victorian atmosphere.

▼28 29►

FLOREAT BATHON
THE BATH ARMS
THE BATH ARMS
Effervescent Mineral Waters
Traditional
RONALD FISHE
Off the Premises.
Splendid Food..

Meeting House Lane (**30**) takes its name from the Friends' Meeting House, which was built here in 1800 and altered and enlarged in 1876; there has been a community of Quakers in Brighton since the 17th century. At the corner of Meeting House Lane opposite the Bath Arms is the Elim Four Square Tabernacle, built by Amon Wilds in 1825 on the site of the earliest Nonconformist chapel in the town (1683).

The Cricketers' Arms (**31**) in Black Lion St is one of the most attractive of Brighton's old inns. It was originally called The Last and Fish Cart, a last being equivalent to 10,000 fish; the doorway was inscribed 'Long time I've looked for good beer, And at "The Last" I've found it here'. In the 1790s, when it was a popular coaching inn, its name was changed by the landlord, Mr Jutton, a great cricket enthusiast. To the right of the pub is the inn yard – the last site of the town pound, and still used as such in the 1860s. To the left is the Derek Carver, a modern inn named after one of the first Protestant martyrs in the reign of Mary Tudor. Derek Carver came to England from Flanders to escape religious persecution; he became a prominent citizen and owner of the Black Lion Brewery (named after the Black Lion of Flanders), which stood on this site. In 1554 he was arrested after attending a prayer meeting in the town, and after several months in Newgate Prison he was burned at the stake at Lewes. He behaved with great courage at his execution, speaking to the assembled crowd and, when the fire was lit, throwing his Bible to the bystanders. His death is commemorated by a plaque on the wall of the new building.

Ship St was built on the area known as the Hempshares (see p. 3), and became known as the Chancery Lane of Brighton because so many lawyers had their offices there. It takes its name from the Old Ship Hotel. This is the oldest inn in Brighton; the earliest reference to it dates from 1559, but its origins may go back further. With the Castle Hotel it became the social centre of the town in the 18th century, when Ship St was one of the main thoroughfares. Its Assembly Rooms, added to the back of the hotel building in 1775, were designed by Robert Golden in an Adamesque style. After the Castle closed balls and concerts continued to be held here, their popularity enhanced by the fact that Mrs Fitzherbert was their patroness for several years. The Assembly Rooms were also used for important town and business meetings, and for property sales. Today the hotel has been modernised and much enlarged, but it remains one of the most popular venues in the town. Ship St still has many of its 18th-century houses; particularly fine are nos. 61–62 (**34**), and no. 69 (**32**), one of the few houses in the centre of the town to be faced with knapped (split) flints, rather than the more traditional materials (see below).

The attractive little 37a, Duke St (**33**), lies hidden in a yard near the junction of Middle St and Duke St. Most unusually it is fronted with boarding; though this is common elsewhere in Sussex it is rare in Brighton, where cottages of this sort were generally faced with cobbles, the most readily available local material (in the case of Brighton these were pebbles picked up from the beach), tarred to protect them from harsh winds and sea spray. Windows and doorways were often surrounded by brick (painted cream to contrast with the black cobbling) to strengthen the structure; brick was used for a whole house only by the rich, as transport costs made it expensive – it had to be brought from the other side of the Downs.

33

▼ 32   34

Ship St Gardens (**35**, **36**), the approach into the Lanes from the west, leads to Prince Albert St, the antique buyers' paradise. Brighton is one of the major centres of Britain's antique trade, and many shops in and around the Lanes sell goods of a variety paralleled in few places outside London; several of them, following the example of the Pavilion, specialise in spectacular pieces of Chinoiserie. Though it is not part of the Lanes proper, Ship St Gardens has the same colourful, intimate atmosphere. Its continuation, Black Lion Lane, is the site of some of the favourite local stories whose point is the narrowness of the Lanes. One of the best known concerns a very fat man who challenged a noted athlete to a race on condition that he could choose the course and be given a start of 10 yards: he chose Black Lion Lane and scored an easy victory, because there was no room for his opponent to overtake him. It is also related that the fugitive Charles II, at one point during his escape from Brighton, was carried down the Lane on the back of a fisherman. They encountered a stout fishwife, and, as he could not pass her and was afraid to go back, the fisherman knocked her down and then climbed over her, bearing his Royal burden to safety.

35

36

Regency Square (**37**) was laid out by Joshua Flesher Hanson in 1818 on land previously known as Belle Vue Fields, where fairs and military reviews were held. A windmill standing in the south-west corner of the field was moved in 1797 to a hill just outside Preston by 36 oxen (a print of this can be seen at Preston Manor), to raise the tone of the area for new residents. Many of the houses have the attractive hooded bow-fronted windows and elegant ironwork balconies characteristic of their period; the architect was probably Amon Wilds. St Albans House, in the south-west corner (now part of the Beach Hotel), was built after the others, having being designed by Amon Wilds' son, A. H. Wilds. Between 1830 and 1837 it was the home of the Duke and Duchess of St Albans; the Duchess had begun her career as the actress Harriet Mellon, and on the death of her first husband, the banker Thomas Coutts, she became the richest woman in England. The Duke of St Albans was 20 years her junior. She left her fortune to her granddaughter, Angela Burdett, who became Baroness Burdett-Coutts, the philanthropist.

Several of the early-19th-century Brighton squares were laid out to face inland; unfortunately the outlook of Russell Square (**38**) has been rather marred by the construction of a multi-storey car park right opposite. In itself however it is charming, with many of the architectural characteristics typical of the town but on a more modest scale than many of the squares. Several of the houses are rather dilapidated, but others have been renovated, for example the one shown here: the bright blue of its balcony is unusual in Brighton, where the dominant colours are cream and pale yellow, and nicely evokes the gaiety of a seaside town.

37 38 ►

'As a means of recreation and health, nothing could be more advantageous, and the beautiful pier will remain as an example to future ages of what speculation has done in the 19th century', declared the Mayor of Brighton at the opening of the West Pier (**39**) in October 1866. The 19th century was the heyday of pier building: piers became fashionable places to promenade at the seaside. The West Pier, designed by Eusebius Birch, was one of the first to be opened – in defiance of opposition from the residents of Regency Square, who felt it would ruin their view of the sea. It was a great success, and attracted large numbers of visitors, besides providing a landing place for steamers. In the early 1890s it was nearly doubled in size by the addition of new landing stages and a concert hall. The pier was renowned for its sideshows which, in 1890, included a display of performing fleas, and a small cannon which was fired at noon every day by the effect of the sun's rays (when the sun shone). Many of the promenaders were visitors at the Grand (**40**) and other smart hotels in this part of the town, so the pier came to be regarded as more 'select' than the Palace Pier. Sadly, one can no longer stroll along the West Pier, as corrosion has made it unsafe. A vigorous preservation campaign has saved this magnificent relic of the Victorian age from demolition, but the cost of repairing its buildings and structure is estimated at £9,000,000. Under West Pier (**41**) are stalls and shops selling all manner of goods for tourists. Looking eastwards along King's Road, one can see the white stucco and ironwork balconies of the Grand Hotel and the concrete of the Brighton Centre. West of the Grand is the red brick and terracotta Metropole Hotel, built in 1888 to a design by Alfred Waterhouse, whose other work includes the Natural History Museum, London. At first it was considered a great eyesore, its harsh colour standing out from the white stucco and pale yellow brick of the other buildings. Some of its most attractive features, the characteristic Waterhouse French pavilion turrets and the little spire on the roof, have been masked by modern additions.

The Grand Hotel: **42**, the Staircase; **43**, the Dining Room, originally the Gentlemen's Coffee Room. By the mid-19th century fewer people wanted to rent a whole house for a stay in Brighton, and hotels were built to cater for their needs. The Grand, designed by J. H. Whichcord, was one of the first to be built and was also the most luxurious and the tallest: when it opened in 1864, the *Brighton Herald* declared that, with its nine stories towering above the other seafront buildings, 'it stands on our cliffs like Saul amidst the men of Israel'. According to the same newspaper report, republished by the hotel in 1977, constituents of the building included 3,500,000 bricks, 450 tons of wrought and cast iron, 1½ acres of glazed tiles, 15 miles of wallpaper, 230 marble chimney pieces, and 12 miles of bell wire; there were 260 rooms and the cost was £160,000. There were many 'Italian' features, including Florentine arches over windows and doorways. This was one of the first hotels in England to be fitted with electric light and lifts, or 'ascending omnibuses', as they were called, for guests. In the 1960s the Grand had fallen into disrepair and was threatened with demolition, but the government refused to countenance such an action and the hotel is now restored, both inside and out, to its Victorian splendour. Other fashionable hotels in the late 19th century included the Norfolk, the Bedford (Dickens' favourite) and the Royal Albion. For the less affluent there sprang up a large number of guest houses and lodging houses, ruled over by that indomitable British institution, the landlady.

Around the Centre from West to East

Building started at Brunswick Square (**45**), in the then tiny village of Hove, in 1824, inspired by the development of Kemp Town (see **53**). The designs were provided by Amon Wilds and C. A. Busby (see p. 13), the leading role being taken by Busby. Together with Brunswick Terrace this estate, Brunswick Town, was intended to be self-supporting; small houses for tradespeople were built adjoining the square, and a church and a closed market were also erected. By the Brunswick Square Act (1830), commissioners were appointed to regulate the estate's affairs; these later became the Hove Commissioners and subsequently Hove Corporation. The part of the Act stipulating that all the houses of the estate be repainted in a uniform colour every three years is still in force. Visitors who stayed in Brunswick Town included Prince Metternich, the exiled Austrian chancellor, who, like several European statesmen and royal personages, took up residence in Brighton after the wave of revolutions that swept through Europe in 1848. Adelaide Crescent (**44**), named after William IV's queen, was begun in 1830; the architect was Decimus Burton. Only 10 houses were constructed at first, the rest of the crescent being left incomplete for 50 years. The difference in design can be clearly seen, the houses added later (those on the eastern side) having much plainer façades and far less charm.

OVERLEAF: the King and Queen Inn (**46**), Marlborough Place, acquired its 'Tudor' appearance in the 1930s, when all its Regency features were destroyed. Before the 1780s it was a farmhouse outside the town proper, and until 1868 it served as the Cornmarket. Formerly barracks backed on to the inn, and drink used to be smuggled to the soldiers through a hole in the wall. The King and Queen, now Henry VIII and Anne Boleyn to fit the Tudor image, were probably originally George III and Queen Charlotte. **47**: one end of Montpelier Crescent. The main sweep of the crescent shows A. H. Wilds' work on its grandest scale. Some of the mansions have his characteristic pilasters with 'Ammonite' capitals, so called because of the resemblance of their volutes to fossil ammonites.

▼**44 4**

The lively Saturday market in Upper Gardener St (**48, 49**) sells all manner of bric-a-brac and second-hand clothes as well as fresh vegetables and fruit, and always attracts flocks of Brighton visitors and residents. This area grew up in the early 19th century. As elsewhere in Brighton, the alignment of the streets was largely determined by the Brighton tenantry laines – arable fields on the edge of the town which were generally subdivided into furlongs separated by narrow pathways known as leakways. When the land came to be built on, speculators tended to develop it a furlong at a time; long rows of houses covered the strips of fields and the leakways became the main streets. The houses were occupied mainly by artisans, who came here in growing numbers after the railway opened. The area was ill-drained and overcrowded, but since the 1970s it has become fashionable. The more derelict terraces have been demolished, and many of the remaining ones have been 'done up'. The cottage character of the houses makes them popular with young families, in preference to the vast Regency houses on the seafront, many of which are now converted into flats for old people and students or used as hotels.

◄ 5

The Royal Crescent (**50**), completed in 1807, was the first of the many early-19th-century housing schemes in Brighton to be planned as a single architectural whole. The building was financed by J. B. Otto, a West Indian speculator; the architect is unknown. The houses form a distinctive and delightful group, standing on the cliff top facing the sea, all fronted with 'mathematical' tiles (see also **19**). They all have four stories, ironwork balconies with bonnet-like canopies and doorways with broken pediments, yet they vary considerably in size and internal structure. When the crescent was finished and its name was being added above the centre houses the workman performing the task leaned back, presumably to examine his work, overbalanced, and fell to his death on the railings below. At one time a statue of the Prince Regent by the sculptor Rossi stood in the middle of the grass enclosure in front of the crescent; Otto erected it to gain favour with the Prince. However it did not have the desired effect, being much disliked by the Regent, and as it was of inferior stone it soon began to crumble, one of the arms disintegrating first, which made people think that it was of Lord Nelson; eventually it was removed (1819).

Much seaside architecture has been influenced by the attraction of the sea itself – people have wanted to be able to see the sea, hence the three-sided squares, the bow windows and the balconies of Brighton. Marine Square (**51**) was built about 1824, inspired, as was so much of the building in this period, by the development of Kemp Town to the east. It was laid out by Thomas Attree, a well-known local figure from a family firm of solicitors whose clients included the Prince Regent (the firm acted for him in the purchases of land for the Pavilion estate). The houses are rather a jumble of details, with a great variety of balconies and verandas, and all with attractive bow windows on the ground and first floors. The eastern side of the terrace has been largely spoiled by modernisation.

Originally the Brighton–Rottingdean road ran along the seafront east of Old Steine, with a stretch of rough fenced ground to the south of it on the cliff edge. When the town spread eastwards this stretch was called East Cliff and, later, Marine Parade. Houses were built along it from about 1800, and despite Victorian and later alteration and rebuilding, many retain their original character. No. 140 (**52**) is one of the most elegant; its attractive balcony is supported on Doric columns, with a railing of plain uprights topped by St Andrew crosses. Like many of the houses on the Parade it was designed by Wilds and Busby.

Lewes Crescent (**53**) is the centre of the grand architectural scheme of Kemp Town, devised by Thomas Read Kemp, a wealthy local landowner and sometime MP for nearby Lewes; he was inspired by Nash's Regent's Park, London, to create a similar development for wealthy residents and visitors in Brighton. Building started in 1823. The main part of the estate consists of Sussex Square, the huge Lewes Crescent (its span is enormous, 840 ft – 200 ft wider than the Royal Crescent in Bath) and, on either side of it, Chichester and Arundel Terraces. Kemp originally intended the estate to be twice its present size, but his money ran out. The architects, Wilds and Busby, were responsible only for the general layout and for the façades; the interiors and backs of the houses were left to be completed by the proprietors, so no two are exactly the same. But the scheme did not take at first, and by 1834 only 34 of the 105 houses were occupied. Kemp went bankrupt and fled the country, just before he was declared an outlaw in Brighton. Later the estate became fashionable. In the mid-19th century, at 1, Lewes Crescent, and the adjacent 14, Chichester Terrace, the Duke of Devonshire entertained Palmerston, Thackeray and Landseer, and Edward VII stayed here with his daughter the Duchess of Fife in 1908. The garden enclosure in front of Lewes Crescent was laid out by the local botanist Henry Philips; the shrubs have been swept into strange shapes by the strong sea wind.

51

Modern developments in Brighton: **54** and **55**, the Marina; **56**, the Brighton Centre. The idea of building a marina in Brighton was first mooted in the 19th century, but it was not until the boom years of the 1960s that plans began to be implemented. The inspiration for the Marina at Black Rock came from Mr Harry Cohen, a local garage owner and keen yachtsman. The original plans were extremely ambitious and included provision for a heliport, a casino, a block of luxury flats and a conference hall, but the escalating costs of the venture (estimated to have risen 1200% in a decade) and vigorous objection by local preservation societies scotched most of these schemes. In fact the Marina has proved to be a very emotive issue, in Brighton and nationally: there were two town polls, two planning enquiries and debates on private members' bills in both Houses of Parliament before the current project was allowed to go ahead. When eventually the Queen opened the Marina in May 1979 only the harbour facilities were complete. These represent a most impressive feat of engineering. The massive harbour walls, encircling 77 acres of sheltered water, make it the largest marina in Europe. It is a thriving concern and has proved popular not only with sailors but also with fishermen (**55**).

Designed by the architects Russell Diplock Associates and built at a cost of over £9,000,000, the Brighton Centre occupies a prime position, on the seafront near the Grand Hotel. It was opened in 1977 as part of Brighton's drive to establish itself as the premier conference venue in Britain. (Conferences are also held at the Dome – where one of the first ever annual conferences, that of the British Association for the Advancement of Science, was held in 1874 – and at the Hotel Metropole's Exhibition Centre.) The Centre provides excellent and highly versatile facilities: the huge main hall seats 2500, with additional retractable seating for another 2500; a second hall holds 800; and there are advanced communication facilities, with 4 camera rooms for the media and 8 interpreting rooms for simultaneous translation.

The Villages from East to West

The small coastal farming community of Rottingdean became a fashionable adjunct to Brighton in the early 20th century, and there was much building along the shore. The village nevertheless retains its peaceful charm in the area around the green, at the north end of the High St. East of the green is St Margaret's church (**58**), mainly 13th century. In 1377 a French raiding party plundered and fired the village, and many villagers were burned alive in the belfry where they had taken refuge. The heat fractured flints in the church walls, and may be the reason for the odd pink and grey colouring of the arches and windows. In this century a group of Americans wanted to buy St Margaret's and take it back to the USA stone by stone; their attempt failed but they built an exact replica in their native Glendale, California, and named it The Church of the Recessional, after the poem by Rudyard Kipling, who lived in Rottingdean, at The Elms, between 1897 and 1903. Timbers (**59**), an excellent example of the conversion of an old Sussex barn into a dwelling, was formerly the main barn of West Side Farm, of which Hillside (**7**) was the farmhouse. Rottingdean Windmill (**57**), a fine 18th-century smock mill, is a prominent landmark on Beacon Hill, west of the village.

OVERLEAF: St Margaret's: the interior. The altar window (**60**), made by Morris & Co, was designed and given by Edward Burne-Jones in 1893 to mark his daughter Margaret's wedding in the church. It depicts the archangels Gabriel, Michael and Raphael, and, below, the Annunciation, Michael slaying the dragon, and the Guardian of little children. Four other windows in the church were also made by the Morris factory to Burne-Jones' designs. The particularly beautiful lancet window in the south side of the tower (**61**) represents the Tree of Jesse and shows Jesse, David, Solomon, Hezekiah, Jonah, and the Virgin and Child. Burne-Jones lived in Rottingdean at North End House from 1880 until his death in 1898; his ashes are buried in the churchyard.

Though Preston village has been obliterated by the spread of Brighton, its identity survives in St Peter's church and Preston Manor. The layout of the delightful gardens of Preston Manor (**62**) is essentially Victorian and Edwardian, but there are some earlier features, such as the sunken garden surrounded by a ha-ha (probably late 18th century) and the walls round the walled garden, which date in part from 1250. Preston Manor House, on the site of a medieval manor, is a mainly 18th-century building, with early-20th-century additions. It now belongs to Brighton Corporation and houses the Thomas-Stanford Museum (named after the Manor's previous owner), a splendid collection of furniture, silver, china and paintings set out so as to give an impression of the house as it was in Edwardian times. The Corporation bought Preston Park in the 1880s for £50,000 to save it from property developers, and today these grounds are full of well-tended flowerbeds and provide such amenities as tennis courts, recreation grounds and playing fields for local residents.

The 13th-century parish church of St Peter (**62**, **63**) is so near to the Manor because in the 16th century the tenant was allowed to add part of the churchyard to his orchard in return for repairing the churchyard walls. Like many Sussex churches, it is of flint with stone dressing. Its chief glory, a wealth of 13th-century wall painting, suffered badly in a fire in 1906, and now only fragments remain: a Nativity scene on the north wall, and the murder of Thomas à Becket on one side of the chancel arch and a detail of the weighing of souls at the Last Judgement on the other. The paintings were whitewashed over in the 16th century and not rediscovered until the 18th.

▼**62** 6

Only a few yards from the busy London–Brighton road lies the village of Patcham. Though now largely swallowed up by Brighton it still retains its own charm, especially in the centre of the village. In the Domesday Book (1086), Patcham is mentioned as Piceham, a manor belonging to William de Warenne; in those days it was a larger and more important settlement than the tiny village of Brighthelmeston which became Brighton. The main part of the village is now contained in the area around the steep Church Hill, on which stands a delightful row of cottages (**66**), some of them dating from the 15th century. They are built of a variety of local materials including brick and flint, with both tiled and slate roofs. In the early 1960s these cottages were threatened with demolition but, thanks to the action of the Patcham Preservation Society and Brighton Corporation, they were spared and skillfully restored, and are now under a preservation order. The church still has its Norman interior, with a (restored) 13th-century depiction of the Last Judgement above the chancel arch.

Patcham Place (**64**), the 'big house' of the village, is Elizabethan in origin but now presents a splendid 18th-century exterior, being faced (unusually for so large a dwelling) with black 'mathematical' tiles, which contrast strikingly with the white of the quoins, the window frames, the cornice and the doorway. In the 17th century the house was owned by the Stapley family, and was the home of Anthony Stapley, one of the signatories of Charles I's death warrant. Now it is a Youth Hostel, and has proved popular with walkers of the South Downs Way.

Southdown House (**65**), an attractive early Georgian house of knapped flint and brick, stands near the end of the London Road.

65

▼ 64 66

PRECEDING PAGES: The town and harbour of New Shoreham, known since 1910 as Shoreham by Sea, were laid out by the Normans about 1100. During the 12th and 13th centuries Shoreham was one of the chief ports of the south coast, and it is still the main port of Sussex. Dominating the town is the striking building of the church of St Mary de Haura (i.e. de Havre, of the harbour), probably the finest medieval church in Sussex (**67**, **68**). It was built between 1100 and 1225, in a mixture of Norman and transitional styles, which admirably demonstrate how the Norman style evolved into Gothic. Originally the church was twice its present length, enormous for a parish church, but the nave lay in ruins by the 17th century – why is uncertain: the damage may have been done during the struggles of the Civil War, or perhaps it was inflicted by a French raiding party in 1628. The tower, 81 ft high, soars above other buildings in the sprawling town, while the weight of the church is supported by magnificent Early English flying buttresses. The congregation is now confined to what was originally the choir. The two magnificent arcades, each of five bays, are of different formations although probably contemporary. The north arcade, shown here, has pillars of alternately round and octagonal columns, their capitals carved with stiff-leaf foliage. The south arcade has compound pillars with column shafts (probably of a slightly later date than the pillars) reaching in an unbroken line to the fine vaulting of the roof.

Empty deck chairs at the end of the day, with the lengthening shadows of the evening sun echoing the stripes on their canvas.

Index to illustrations

(Numbers refer to illustrations)

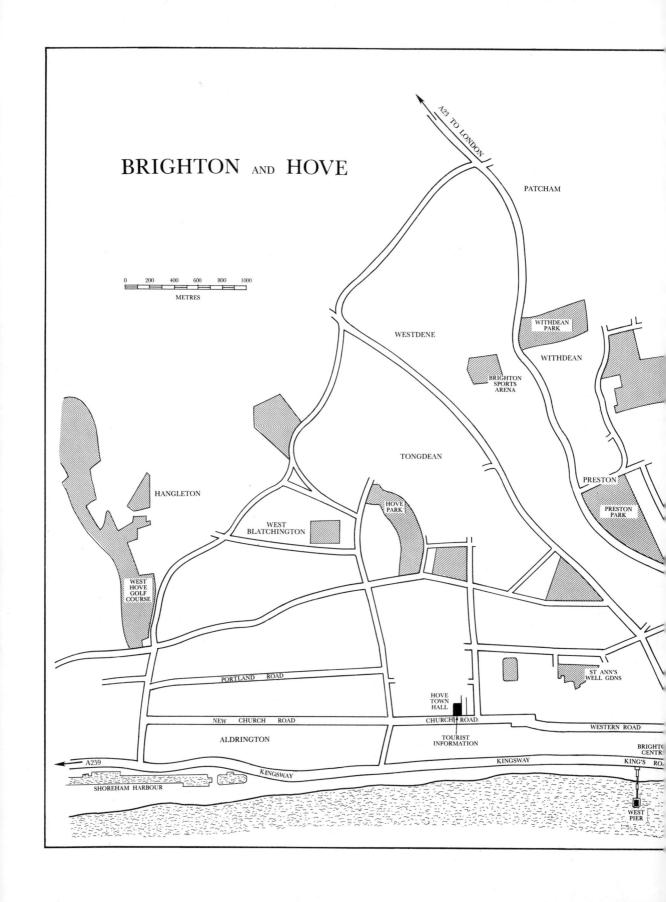